Forward

We at Apricot Press are always striving to bring only the best products to you, the reading public. In our booger humor, we use only the finest ingredients, the funniest premises, the sharpest punch lines, the edgiest sarcasm, and yet, as you know, you can always count on our jokes to be 100% safe and non-carcinogenic. That's why we are so disappointed when we hear that one of our readers spent his or her hard-earned money on substandard, even dangerous humor from one of our competitors. Besides the fact that it's usually not funny, other publishers' humor may also cause the degenerative diseases, which lead to heart attacks, manic depression, or gout; it could even kill you. That's why we implore you to buy only pure "grade A" Apricot Press booger humor. Accept no substitutes.

More Forward

As the title suggests, the subject of this book is "worrying." Unfortunately, the author couldn't think of enough stuff on the topic to fill an entire book. (Hey, you should try writing a whole book filled with nothing but good material on only one topic sometime; it's not as easy as it looks.) Fortunately, many of my readers probably won't even notice. However, if you happen to be one who DOES notice those kinds of things, and if it really bothers you, feel free to skip the

The Fine Art of
Worrying

The Official Guide Book for Worry Warts

Ben Goode

Illustrated by
David Mecham

The Truth About Life ™

Published by:
Apricot Press
Box 1611
American Fork, Utah
84003

books@apricotpress.com
www.apricotpress.com

ISBN 1-885027-21-4

Cover Design & Layout by David Mecham
Printed in the United States of America

parts that aren't about the subject of worrying. Hopefully, that will make you feel better. If it doesn't, we suggest you call somebody like the Pope if you want to complain. While the Vatican probably won't do anything to solve the problem, someone there may be able to at least give you perspective.

Ben Goode

Contents

Worriers: Here are a couple of pages to get you going

What if:

God had no sense of humor?

Sleeping made you tired?

Men were as complicated as women?

Stupidity was contagious?

Abused cars really did conspire to get even?

Dessert was illegal?

Bathing made you shrink?

Your mom knew all about everything you do?

Somebody screwed your eyes in backwards?

Your teeth were really only marshmallows?

The voices in your head started insisting that you lick a bunch of car tires?

You got the "Barney" theme song stuck in your head for an entire decade?

Your wife could read your thoughts?

Your husband could read your thoughts?

You cut your tax auditor off in traffic?

The government sends you a 30-day invoice for your share of the national debt?

In the next life, for entertainment, they play home movies of all the stupid things you've done?

Mosquito bites itched on the inside?

In the next life we all get to come back as a rodent...or a lawyer?

Your kids found out about everything you did when you were a kid?

The large meteor speeding toward earth is made of dog doo doo?

You and your friends were the ones paying for all the government freebies?

The extra-terrestrials are finally starting to get bored with us?

Worry #23498
Is that baseball mit one of my relatives?

 Mega Worrying

People today are worried. We worry that the economy will go into the tank, causing us to get laid off from our job as quality control tester at the dental floss foundry. We worry that our son or daughter won't make the team or cheerleading squad and we will have to spend a mountain of money to bribe coaches or to hire a hit man to take out some of the competition. We worry that our taxes will get pulled for an audit and that the IRS will notice that we deducted the cost of 138 Big Macs as a research expense. We worry that someday soon pigs will fly causing all kinds of unlikely events to happen. Let's face it; we have lots to worry about.

Things that should make us worry

While it's true that some of us worry about things we shouldn't, there are scads of things that we SHOULD be worried about, yet we're not. It could be that we're not aware; maybe we're preoccupied with other, less important worries; or, maybe we're just plain stupid. And this has me worried. Many of us need to worry about the fact that if we should fall down, the rumble would register on regional earthquake measuring devices. Most of us should worry that in order to pass through our arteries, red corpuscles have to do the limbo rock between blobs of blubber and waxy build up. All of us should be constantly worried that our beliefs and values might offend someone who blindly hates people like us and yet who is very sensitive. Global warming, the size of our automobile, and the psychological health of our pets should be constantly on our minds, as should the fear that a neighbor will report us for being abusive because we asked our children to turn off MTV so they can clean up their cartridges of violent video games.

Things about which we could worry

Because we know there are so many of you who have a biological need to be in a constant state of worry, and because if you aren't worrying you don't know what to do with your brain, which can cause boredom and, which could lead to work, I need to give you a few extra things that you COULD be worrying about so you don't just go out and watch reality TV. For example, take gravity. What if all of a sudden it quit working, or even worse, went into reverse? Your peanut butter and jam sandwich would now land upside down on the ceiling! Ponder that! And what about ground water? What if it escaped? What if it fled to higher ground? It might become tree water or something, and shouldn't we all take a few hours each day and worry about hair loss?

What if there was no math? Many of you might think, "great. Now we have less homework and the geek segment of the population will have to find some games where they learn to interact with actual people."

Oh, the shallowness! If there were no math, there would be no way to accurately tabulate the results of studies on weasel migration, no way to count public opinion polls, and we would be forced to wonder which contestant got voted off "Survivor."

How about this: shouldn't we worry how depressed third world dictators must feel? Imagine what it would be like to have to hole up in some godforsaken bladder of the world on a throne surrounded by beautiful women in chains catering to your every whim, while behind every bush lurks a relative of someone you tortured who wants to kill you. Imagine how you would feel knowing that if your regime is ever overthrown, the whole world will know about the corpses of the 11 million political opponents your thugs have tortured and killed, which could cause the entire world except for the movie stars to look unfavorably upon your regime. Plus, you have to keep up a constant flow of drug profit bribes and maintain an innocent front to stay in the good graces of the fraternity of other third world dictators who make up the U.N. So you see, there are plenty of things to worry about. Even if you are someone who is worry disadvantaged, certainly, before you finish this book, you will be able to find something cool that even YOU can worry about. And if you are a polished, veteran worrier, reading this book will make your dandruff multiply even faster and your fingernails disappear and you will probably worry if the two are somehow connected. I wonder if that spot on my tennis shoe is cancerous.

Things a cow should worry about...

Will the farmer have cold hands?

What if I don't want to be milked twice-a-day?

Where does hamburger come from?

What do you suppose happened to all the bugs you knew were living in this grass?

Could there be more to my life than just eating and being milked?

Why did they put all my friends in that big truck?

Are any of my relatives baseball mits?

What about shoes?

Things a tree should worry about...

Is that woodpecker coming over here?

Would I make a good cellar door? Hope chest?

Is that smoke over there a forest fire?

If a monster comes, I can't run away.

If they call me a knot head, is that OK?
Should I be insulted?

Is that sound in the distance a Suzuki 120
or a chain saw?

What if I decide I don't want birds in my hair?

What if I get tired and want to lie down?

Do the other trees consider me a sap?

Things a hot dog should be worrying about...

What am I <u>really</u> made of?

Will all these preservatives be bad for my blood pressure?

What future is there in being a wiener?

What if I want to change careers? Life styles? Food groups?

Since we all pretty much look and taste the same, how can I be my own person?

What are they planning to do with that pointed stick?

If pondering my purpose in life makes me suicidal, considering I'm a wiener, are there any good alternatives?

What are the odds of me being used in a wiener-friendly recipe?

Are there any wiener advocacy groups?

Isn't there a good way to wear mustard and sauerkraut during bun season?

Worry #4278
Will the children remember exactly
where on this beach they buried me?

2 What Should I Worry About?

Psychologists often point out that there are good worries and there are bad worries. In spite of our most determined efforts, it's impossible for most of us to worry about everything in the universe. Most of us, who are not almighty and all knowing, at times must pick and choose our worries. Therefore, we want to give you some guidelines, to make it easier to choose your worries and still appear to be sane. The best way to do this is to use electric shock therapy; however, since this is only a book, instead of shock therapy, we will attempt to shock you with words on paper. The following is a partial list of things you probably shouldn't worry about. Any of you out there who have the basic intelligence to perspire will easily recognize that worrying about stuff like this could cause people to be careful when choosing their words in your presence.

Stuff about which it would be pointless to worry:

(If you are worrying about things like these, you are really going the extra mile.)

1. What color is the inside of my colon?

2. Am I taller from my feet to my head – or from my head to my feet?

3. Do these high-topped P.F. Flyers match my pajamas?

4. Is my immune system planning to attack my boy friend?

5. Can that girl over there read my thoughts?

6. If I die tonight, will my cat miss me?

7. Does that cloud over there look more like a swan or Homer Simpson?

That was all of those we could think of. The following is a partial list of things you probably SHOULD worry about:

A bunch of stuff it could be healthy to worry about:

1. By the time I get the car door open will I be able to hold my breath long enough to swim to the top of this lake I just drove into?

2. Did I just throw the grenade or the pin?

3. Is the object I just put into my mouth a lettuce wrap...or hemlock?

4. Will the children remember exactly where on this beach they buried me?

5. Would that furry object 6-inches from my nose be a skunk's backside or a fur-lined license plate?

6. Why does this pork chop taste like my cat?

7. Does my loan officer know that it was my 4-year-old daughter who beat up her 6-year-old son at school today?

8. Is this garbage truck that is parked on my head planning to stay here for the entire lunch hour?

9. Could that sound I hear be the wind whistling through my satellite dish or a bunker buster bomb headed for my palace?

10. Did I give permission for my home to be used as a movie set, or are these real aliens?

Additional perspective:

Things a diaper should be worried about:
(Fill in the blanks)

1 _____

2 _____

Things a thermometer should be worried about:
(Fill in the blanks)
1 _____

2 _____

3 _____

4 _____

What a Kleenex should be worried about:
(Fill in the blanks)

1 _____

2 _____

3 _____

Things a nail should be worried about:
(Fill in the blanks)

1 _____

2 _____

3 _____

Stuff a hand grenade should worry about:
(Fill in the blanks)

1 _____

2 _____

3 _____

Worry #4758
What if there's a land mine in my scratch box?

 # Health Strategies to Affect Your Worrying

Some of my readers may not be aware that I am a health expert. (Some of my readers would probably not be aware if they were being neutered with a power sander, but that's not the point.) Bon-a-fide health experts like myself understand the connection between exercise and stress, which is, you can't be performing at your frantic best like a raccoon in the middle of a rush hour freeway, if you are feeling as hammered as a tomato in a rock-polishing machine. Therefore, staying in tip-top health is essential.

I know, even without you telling me this, that many of you are concerned about your health, because you spend upwards of $80 billion a year on it.

Unfortunately, much of this money goes to poorly thought-out strategies, weakly bound books, and sadly, some of it to right out quackery, (And in case you didn't know, there are some pretty unsavory people in the field of quackery.). So, I figure if you're going to spend hard earned cash on outright medical fraud, rather than have your money go to slimy, unsavory characters, if you buy your quackery from us and our program turns out to be bogus, at least your money will be going to some really fine people, and I might add, to people who really need it. It won't be wasted on sleazy dirt bags who would steal your wallet if given the chance. We would never steal your wallet because we think there's a chance we can get you to fork over your credit cards willingly. So, to that end, here are a few health strategies we hope you'll find interesting--and we'll find lucrative.

Some health strategies of dubious value

1. Vitamins by the kilo

This operates on the theory that if one aspirin will help get rid of a little headache, 500 aspirins will totally obliterate it, maybe prevent another headache for eternity[1] or longer. So, obviously, we recommend you take lots of vitamins, vitamins of all kinds. You can't

---

[1] Don't misunderstand. We are NOT recommending that you take 500 aspirins, especially not without physician's supervision, and even then not without trying it out on your cat first.

get too many vitamins. The more vitamins I eat, I figure, the more hamburgers, bacon cheeseburgers, and pork rinds I can eat. The way I see it, 4 hamburgers equals 4 vitamins; if I eat 6 vitamins, I can eat 6 banana splits, and so forth.

It stands to reason that if this strategy works with vitamins, it would probably also work with such common products as make up, fertilizer, mouthwash, energy drinks, deodorant, and hair spray.

2. The action exercise program
Some of you have seen the play, THE MUSIC MAN. In this play, the main character, Humphrey Bogart, plays a con man who sold band instruments to children in this high school somewhere in Seattle or Northern Africa. Because he is a con man and, therefore, has no idea how to actually teach the kids to play the instruments, he uses the concept of visualization to help them imagine themselves playing the instruments as a way to keep them from wearing drapes as clothes and fleeing Austria. And the moral of the story is that the fraud actually works! At least it gets him the beautiful babe, and he gets to keep the money. So, we can conclude that the power of the human mind, at least some of them, is pretty amazing.

So, by using this same principle in YOUR exercise program, we figure you can become as fit and good looking as just about anybody who ever exposed herself in a rock video—even if you're built like a sea cucumber, if you're 200 pounds over weight, even if you're 90 years old and as wrinkled as laundry that spent the weekend in a motionless dryer. Here's how the technique works: If you hate exercising, just take a few minutes each day and visualize yourself working out on an exercise bike, a treadmill, or some other monotonous machine. Realize, of course, that since the monotony of this may put you right to sleep, or into a hypnotic trance or something, you should probably not try it while you're driving or operating heavy equipment. If you use this visualization technique long enough, one of two things will happen: either you will literally visualize yourself into shape or you will not.

Now, if you want to take your fitness to a completely fanatical level, I have another program I call "the frantic gerbil technique," and it's highly technical.

3. The Frantic Gerbil Technique

Although I have no data to backup this theory, it seems logical to me that since this entire program is only in your head, if you want to, you could imagine these images moving like a squirrel on an electric fence. Logically then, if you double the speed of the images in your mind, this will cut your exercise time in half. I'll bet if you were to spend 10 minutes visualizing yourself swimming like a guppy in a tsunami, that this 10 minute visualization could be every bit as effective as 20 minutes of imagining yourself swimming at a normal workout pace.

Now, I know, some of you have already spotted a potential problem here. Instead of concentrating on YOUR OWN exercise program, some of you perverts out there will want to visualize Brittney Spears or Christine Aguilera doing THEIR aerobics. This will not work. Anyone can plainly see that they don't need the exercise. Furthermore, I suspect that some of you clowns will visualize Popeye, Mr. Bean, or Roseanne Barr on a high-speed hamster-wheel and make the whole exercise a big joke. If you won't take things seriously, how can I help you?

Another potential risk of this type of program would present itself if you were to visualize yourself taking amphetamines, appetite suppressants, NoDoz, or heroin to speed up your metabolism. This, too, is a bad idea. Remember: these are gateway drugs which often lead to harder stuff like potato chips, sausage, bacon, and ice cream sundays or maybe even dolphin meat.

4. Mega-Resistance Training

Strength, or resistance training has also become a staple with many people who hate to run. The problem for many would-be weightlifters is that getting the right equipment can be expensive. For example, gym memberships can cost hundreds of dollars. Even if you go with a paying friend who sneaks you in as a guest to a different club every day, or hop the fence at a nice motel while the concierge has his head turned, eventually you are bound to get caught and the only place left for you to sneak into could be gyms or motels as far away as Pakistan. Even buying a membership is usually not the answer because most people I know use their memberships only a couple of times then wind up paying on a dead horse for the next 25 years. This can be outrageously expensive.

Buying your own equipment can cost a fortune too. Why, I know one couple, who spent $200.00 to buy this used set of asbestos abdominal flexors and while they were moving to a new apartment, one of their neighbors who was trying to help carry them up the stairs accidentally dropped the machine on his foot and wound up suing them for a million bucks.

Since these are negative things, we're going to avoid discussing them and instead talk about your cholesterol, which can be good or bad. Since science has found all this bad stuff out about cholesterol, and we certainly have no idea how they figured it out, in fact, we think there's a very real possibility they're making this all up and having a good laugh at our expense. And since we're talking about expenses, they're raking in billions from us while they laugh, and what could possibly be more healthy and stress-relieving than a good laugh while raking in dough? Doesn't it make you feel good to be a part of something so healthy and successful?

So we join you, the health-gimmick buying public in giving our hearty endorsement to good health.

Here are a few things your cat probably should worry about:

1. What are those boys doing with that fire cracker? ...that gunny sack? Etc...?

2. What if there's a land mine in my scratch box?

3. If times got really rough for the big people, which would they eat first: me or their kids?

4. Should I be concerned if my owner schedules an appointment for me with the vet?

5. Were any of these roadside fur flapjacks close relatives of mine?

6. What if it becomes fashionable for teenagers to put cats feet on their key chains?

7. If everyone becomes a vegetarian, what will I eat?

Here are a few things that would be appropriate for a fish to worry about:

1. What if I forget how to swim?

2. If I decide to do the backstroke just for fun, will someone flush me down the toilet?

3. When all these other fish have to go, where do they do it?

4. How do I tell the difference between food and bait?

5. How can I improve my position in the food chain?

6. Why do I not rate my own plural?

Here are a few things that are appropriate for a chicken to worry about:

1. What part of me is the nugget?

2. Where is the farmer taking my children?

3. Since I have such a small brain, will I be at a disadvantage when I need higher thinking skills?

4. How does such a big egg get out?

5. Do I have lips?

6. Should we hold a funeral for a chicken sandwich?

7. What if I start craving a chicken sandwich?

8. What if I become a chicken sandwich?

9. If they call me a "big chicken," is that a good thing or a bad thing?

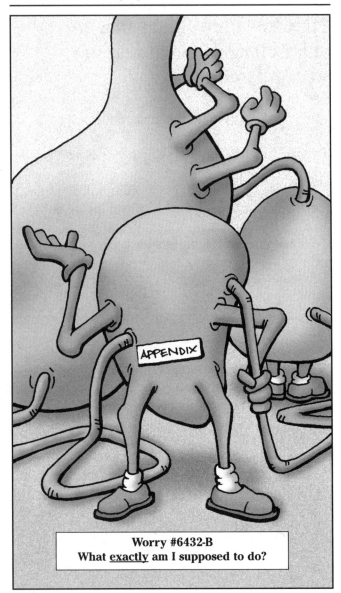

Worry #6432-B
What <u>exactly</u> am I supposed to do?

4

The Next Chapter

As most of you know, there is worrying and then there is serious worrying. Most of us know someone who is so good that when he finally gets a raise, he worries the company can't afford it. When her cancer tests come back negative, she starts worrying that the surgeon will be disappointed. When he loses 15 pounds, he worries that he might have offended some fat cells in the process.

I know there are many who admire all the highly trained, very good worriers out there and wonder, "Could I ever worry like that?" Many of you already do and therefore don't need my help, but if we make a big deal about that, no one will buy this book, and then I will have to worry about finding a real job, so work with me here. Where were we? Oh, yeah. The question is, "could I ever worry like that?" And the answer, of course, is: "do you know a good shrink?" But since so many of my readers I know seem to enjoy worrying, I have taken this question as seriously as an adolescent male takes a dare to see how many marsh-mallows he can stuff up his nose. Therefore, we will now address the subject of "How to worry."

How to Worry

You know, in my career I have written some pretty silly things and tried to pass them off as serious useful information, but this is one topic that may be too lame for even me. Since if there really is anyone out there who really does not know how to worry, they are way beyond any help from me, I'm going to bag that and talk about cat owners.

Cat Owners

Over the years I have observed there are just a few classes of people who have absolutely no concept of humor whatsoever. At the top of this short list, along with political special interest groups and Bella Abzug, are cat lovers. Like me, I'm sure that most of you have spent a lifetime wondering how it is possible that these people can survive without a functioning sense of humor. Most of you out there, if forced to choose between a huge pile of money and your sense of humor, without any thought at all would quickly choose the money. Of course, that is only because with enough money, you can buy your own comedian, but for the rest of us who have no pile of money, the only way we survive is because of our sense of humor. "So how do these people do it?" We wonder. I'm sure I don't know, but just in case you doubt your own worrying competence, here are a few random suggestions:

A Few Random Suggestions:

1. Never take cheese as a cure for your constipation. I tried eating a bunch of it once when I was plugged up and then, to make matters worse, I ate a bunch of cherries afterward. Let's change the subject and move on to number 2.

2. Don't wash your hair in light beer and battery acid.

3. Wherever possible, avoid partying with biting ants.

4. Imagine that worrying is like a tank of gas. If you spend time wallowing in it, no one will want to sit by you in church.

So, hopefully these suggestions will be of some value to you even though they have nothing to do with worrying. Nevertheless, they are pretty good suggestions.

Things your wart should be worried about:

1. What is the doctor planning to do with that electrode?

2. Will the top of my head grow back after she bites it off?

3. Why don't I have any friends?

4. If I do make some friends, will they burn them off too?

5. Why don't I look any better on a toad?

6. Since I'm a virus, and, technically, a virus is an animal, why isn't anyone fighting for my rights?

7. After they burn me off, what will become of me? Will I be happy?

8. After they burn me off, who will take care of me?

9. Since I have no brain, who is doing this thinking?

10. Since I have no brain, how am I able to ask these questions?

Things your brain should worry about:

1. Am I damaged?

2. Am I retarded?

3. What if I send a message to the nerves to tell the feet to stop before they walk in front of a cement truck and the nerves forget to mention it?

4. What if they remove this fluid I'm floating in and replace it with gravel?

5. What if they remove this fluid I'm floating in and replace it with methane gas?

6. What if they remove this fluid I'm floating in and replace it with Mountain Dew?

7. What if they remove this fluid I'm floating in and replace it with Jack Daniels?

8. Does he love me for myself or just for my body?

9. What if he makes me watch a night of TV again?

10. If I tell the lungs how disgusting they are, will they still send me oxygen?

Appropriate things for a teenager to worry about:

1. What if Dad forgets to pay my cell-phone bill?

2. What if Dad leaves the house with the car keys in his pocket?

3. When Mom and Dad leave town, will they leave a baby sitter?

4. What if Mom or Dad get to the mailbox before I do on the day my report card comes?

5. What if someday I'm no longer a teenager and I have to take care of myself?

6. Does everybody think I'm a dork?

7. What if Mom and Dad are smarter than I think?

8. What if Mom and Dad know what they're talking about?

9. What if they're right about everything?

10. What if all these things I think are cool, turn out to be really stupid?

A few things your appendix should be worried about:

1. How do I look?

2. What <u>exactly</u> am I supposed to do?

3. If I decide I want to try to make something of myself, what are my options?

4. If I swell up and burst, what happens next?

5. Will I ever have any friends?

6. Let's say I came up with a bunch of money, would that improve my life?

7. Let's say life places you in a situation which requires "guts," what if you have none, but you are one?

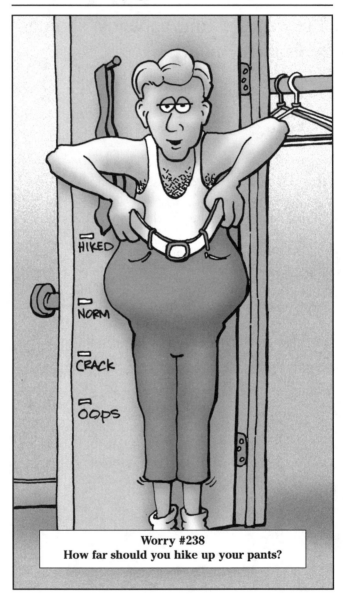

Worry #238
How far should you hike up your pants?

 Fashion Tips for Men With Bellies

One of the most widespread worries today is looking sharp when you have a belly. Being a veteran belly person, I speak with some authority when I say that you should never rub vinegar on chapped lips and if you insist on snorkeling over the dam, use a little caution. But getting back to the main point, a belly poses some unique worries. For example:

1. How do you keep your shirt tucked in?

2. What are you supposed to do when you lose a button right at the widest part of your belly and you're someplace where you can't change clothes?

3. How are you supposed to tie your shoes?

4. How far should you hike up your pants?

A. Just to the bottom side of your belly which causes the belt to curl downward, or...

B. Hiked up on top of your belly so your appearance shouts to the world, "Hey look, a well-dressed alien dweebe?" (I should point out here that your pants level is only an issue until you reach age 72, after which safety and balance trump fashion consciousness. Around age 72, you will need to hike them up for support and balance.

Then there is an unrelated fundamental question. Are you OK having the public see how your abdominal muscle fibers have shrunk over the past decades like hemorrhoidal tissue soaking in Preparation H mixed with grape slush, and that this formerly firm mass has transmogrified until it is now the consistency of canned cream of chicken soup, and that the only thing keeping your middle from settling down around your ankles is a good, wide leather belt? If you answered "no" to this question, I have no idea what to do; however, I would like to address the 4 challenges listed above within a high fashion context. I would also like to be able to turn inconsiderate drivers into mold spores or stereo bass notes, but, on second thought, since I can't do either one, I think I'll have another bacon cheeseburger and deal with reality.

Dealing with reality

Because of pride and social pressure, if you are like most guys with bellies, you've been trying for 30 years to get rid of that thing and in spite of a plethora of diets and everything else you do, it just keeps expanding like a hamster's genealogy, like your bladder during a <u>Lord of the Rings</u> movie, like the cost of a federal program for senior citizens. So let's be realistic. This year's diet and exercise program will be as effective at reducing the size of your belly as an order of French fries are at getting rid of zits, or as the Bar association is at getting rid of crooked lawyers, or like public education is at reducing stupidity. So, we say, "bag this" and do something, which will at least make you THINK you are looking good.

How to THINK you look good

At first, I tried racking my brain to come up with some ideas that will help guys with bellies. After considerable thought, the best I could do was imagine a girdle made of duct tape that could hold your belly in, which would let you wear the same clothes everybody else does. But since squishing all your inside goo under so much pressure could make your voice squeak, I decided to try a more scientific approach. We mailed out a questionnaire to 500 random women to get empirical data. We asked the question: "WHAT COULD A GUY WITH A BELLY WEAR THAT WOULD MAKE YOU WANT HIM AS BAD AS YOU

WANT A LAUNDRY BASKET FILLED WITH CHOCOLATE MOUSSE?"

After a couple of months of waiting, since not so much as one of our questionnaires ever came back, all we could figure was that random women must not have very strong opinions, either that or else they were so dingy they sent them back to random addresses or something. In any case it was clear that random women clearly weren't the way to go, and since we needed to get this done before I became senile, we decided to question a different type of woman.

We decided what we needed were women with analytical minds, women who could take charge, women with husbands who had bellies. So, naturally we selected an expert panel made up of the women in our office. While they were discussing the question, and I might add having about as much fun as a toad at a fly convention, and while I was waiting for them to finish discussing it, since they were hooting like a flock of owls walking barefoot over hot coals, I made a couple of my own observations: If you're a guy with a belly, and since women seem to either ignore you, like the ones in the survey, or make fun of you, like the ones in my office, why not just do fashion YOUR way? Why not wear stuff you would have designed if you were the fashion police? Concentrate purely on comfort. I would argue that if you wear stuff that feels comfortable, that feeling of relaxation will come across to the people you meet and they will want to check your pulse to see if you're still alive.

So then, finally the ladies in my office got themselves composed enough to weigh in on the subject. The fashion police here in my office have five recommendations:

1. Robyn says she would go with sweats. They are comfortable, and you can go nearly anywhere in them. Just be careful when you bend over to fix something. Check your rear-view mirrors (no pun intended). Crack kills.

2. Erin suggests Dickies. Since most of you will get around to wearing them anyway, eventually, if they don't thrill you at this point, just be patient. Apparently, when you get a little older, they will grow on you.

3. Kelsey recommends '70's style short shorts. She says they look great on guys with bellies, especially if they also have bird legs or varicose veins. (I should note: she may have been being sarcastic.)

4. Dana thinks a bathrobe would be trendy. She says she has seen lots of old guys with bellies go in some pretty unusual places in their robes, and if, heaven forbid, you should get into an accident, have a heart attack or a stroke, you will save precious time by arriving at the hospital already appropriately dressed.

5. Blow everyone's mind and wear a kilt.

If you are normal, you worry about these things:

1. Noticing, as you put it into your mouth, that your toothbrush is already wet.

2. Having to sit through a series of feminine hygiene commercials-or worse- while watching TV with your kids.

2. Having a conversation with a lady who has a booger flapping in the breeze of her left nostril the whole time.

3. Sitting down on a wet toilet seat.

4. Seeing the I.R.S. number on your caller I.D.

5. Feeling a draft in the area of your fly towards the end of a presentation to a large, formal group.

6. Putting your foot into your boot and feeling something squishy.

7. Seeing Congress get together in bi-partisan harmony to approve spending an enormous pile of our money.

8. Contemplating a long ride in a car with someone with whom last time you had close contact, had terminal moose breath.

9. Realizing that the three kernels making up the last spoonful of cereal this morning aren't kernels of cereal at all, but are plump weevils.

10. Watching a toddler you don't know crawl around and forage for items on the floor of the bus depot.

11. Noticing a murder is taking place in one of your photos when you get your pictures back from the developer.

12. Realizing your wife's birthday was two days ago.

13. Pondering precisely where that egg you're eating actually comes from.

Things a lawyer should be worried about:

1. When everyone becomes a lawyer, who will we sue?

2. How do they get away with showing insulting movies like "Jaws?"

3. If the other lawyers' clients all get off, will they restrain themselves from killing or stealing from me out of professional courtesy?

4. Should I have high self-esteem even though I make a career of sucking the life out of our economy and hastening society's moral decline?

5. Why are people constantly confusing me with ticks, leeches, bats, and other parasites?

Things an Apricot Press graphic designer should be worried about:

1. What if he gave me this project as a big joke?

2. Because I can come up with these strange drawings from my head, does that mean I'm insane? Delusional?

3. If my entire professional portfolio is pretty much booger humor, will this actually enhance my career?

4. Who else would hire me?

5. What is the likelihood that 2000 years from now one of my paintings will be found by archeologists on the wall of a cave or a tomb?

6. What if I spend weeks getting all this work ready to go and then my computer crashes?

 Technology Induced Worry

I am a recovering technophobe. While a virtual plethora of new inventions have thrilled our ever-expanding nerd population, many standard normal people think lots of this stuff is stupid. Some are even so irritated trying to figure out which buttons to push on all this junk that they are considering a return to running naked through the trees eating roots and berries. Every time some new gadget comes out, while thousands of geeks and dweebes are hyperventilating like prairie dogs in labor, the sane segment of the population is thinking sarcastically, "Oh joy, another operating manual."

For example, let's examine the microwave oven. Most of us living today have forgotten what life was like without the microwave oven. While this is understandable for those younger people who weren't alive in the '70's, for the rest of you, this is pathetic. You should be checked for Alzheimers. But that's not the point. Amazingly, only two short decades ago, we had to find other ways to heat the leftovers in the fridge so we could get them out and realize that they smelled like a dead raccoon and were probably filled with microorganisms waiting for an opportunity to turn our brains into a pumpkin. While most of us would not want to go back to the good old days when there were no microwaves and we had to find other ways to dry our socks or to make a toad pop, I should point out how this one invention has increased stress levels.

A case in point: You know perfectly well that nobody besides you ever cleans up the inside of the microwave at work, and so you have to worry that the rotting biodegradable filth on the inside will someday migrate to your left-over lasagna and cause you to go into convulsions. Since your mother doesn't work there, this worry can make you as stressed as a rabbit at a dog show. And the microwave isn't the only modern convenience that causes stress.

Consider the nail gun. A person who doesn't know any better might think, "Hey, with this cool tool, one guy can take the place of 3 or 4 who used to have to pound every individual nail by hand, or if they were really psycho, with their foreheads." You might think the nail gun was a stress reliever, but you would be wrong if you overlooked the stress brought on when, while you were putting the plywood onto your roof and you had to holler for someone to bring an old fashioned claw hammer all the way up the ladder to pull the nail out of your foot that you shot in there when you were holding down the trigger and accidentally bumped the end, and then you had the added stress of having to drive like a baby duck fleeing an alligator migration to get to the hospital before you bled to death, all the while operating the clutch AND brake with only one working foot.

Another modern example of a gadget which looks harmless enough, but which has caused great stress is the dishwasher. For generations, whenever people would make a meal, someone had to clean it up and wash the dishes or Mom would get mad. At first glance, it looks as though being able to just put all the dirty dishes into the dishwasher and turn it on would be less time consuming and stressful than standing over the sink for an hour washing them by hand. You would think this until you remember that now days, after a meal, everyone expects you to walk over to the dishwasher, open it up, and put your own plate, bowl, glass, and spoon into the appropriate spot, even if you are at someone else's house and the woman in charge demands to have her dishwasher loaded so the cups make patterns that match the wallpaper. Compared to the old way of just having the women in the house clean up the mess; this is a lot of work. Thus, dishwashers cause a lot of stress.

Finally, a philosophical look at the common, house-hold nuclear reactor, will give us an idea how, instead of relieving stress and worry, so many of these modern so-called conveniences can actually complicate our lives and cause even more worry.

The following are more examples of modern inventions, which, instead of eliminating stress actually bring it on: THE SMART BOMB, THE LASER GUIDED MISSILE, THE CELL PHONE, THE COMPUTER VIRUS, THE LIE DETECTOR, THE GOLF CLUB, THE SINGING-MOVING GIFT FISH, THE LAWN MOWER, THE ALARM CLOCK, THE RECTAL EXAM, THE FAX MACHINE, THE MAIL BOX, THE MICRO-PHONE, THE UNIVERSAL GYM, THE FLAT TIRE, THE NEIGHBOR'S DOG, THE HIGH DIVING BOARD, THE TAX AUDIT, SUSHI, THE EARLY PREGNANCY TEST, THE PARA-CHUTE, and THE MOTHER-IN-LAW, just to name a few.

There, hopefully, this will prove that just inventing more gadgets does not, in reality, simplify our lives or reduce stress.

Stuff a famous actor or musician should be worried about:

1. When I am no longer famous, attractive, or rich enough to buy them stuff, will these people hanging around still be my friends?

2. What if the majority of all these adoring fans who go to the trouble to write me flattering letters and E-mails are mentally ill or bored from too much time on their hands?

3. What if the perverse lifestyle and dope I've smoked over the years has warped my brain leaving me unable to comprehend normal, healthy morality?

4. What if the fact that I am shallow and vain is obvious to everyone but me?

5. Will magazines still want me on their covers when I can no longer afford to have my skin tightened?

6. What if 99% of my fans genuinely aren't interested in my position on political issues?

7. What if some day those little people in military uniforms were no longer willing to fight for my right to treat them condescendingly?

Worry #1238-A
If I do the backstroke just for fun, will
someone flush me down the toilet?

7

Stress Relievers

Recently, my son got a fish tank. I had never realized what a stress reliever a little tropical fish could be. When I was growing up, we always viewed things like pets and aquariums filled with fish pretty much as food storage, but, thanks to my son's hobby, I've been given a new perspective. The relaxing, bubbling sound of air fluttering while trying to push its way up through the algae, the gold fish being eaten by the eel, the soothing sound of your child whining because you're making him clean the filters, all these can make a person forget his or her stresses and truly relax.

Even though it seems as though most of you choose to live your life in the eye of the hurricane, symbolically dodging flying boards, shattered window glass, riding lawn mowers and airborne Asian pot-bellied pigs, we know there are times when your therapist recommends you have some kind of diversion to delay the big snap. So, in order to delay the moment when all you book-reading friends of mine, who live your lives on the edge, decide it's time to get a serious criminal record just so you can have an all expense paid vacation at the nut house, here are a few more stress-relieving ideas for you to try...or maybe just visualize.

Stress-relieving strategy #1

Stand relaxed; while facing your spouse and teen-aged daughter, wiggle your fingers and take a deep breath. Then, carefully pry the cell phone out of your daughter's hands, and lay it gently on top of the pineapple chunks. Then, turn on the blender. We call this stress-reduction technique "power call forwarding", and trust me; it will make you feel better.

Stress-relieving strategy #2

During the nightly news, right after the part where the anchor-person tells us that housing starts are off 4%, the stock market is down 120 points, and interest rates are climbing, but just before the part about the plane crash, 4-car pile up, and the expert explaining why animals are nice and people are bad, or in the middle of the latest sick, perverted reality program, place your TV set on the pavement right behind your '84 Dodge pickup. Slowly back your truck up until your tire is firmly on top of your set. Now, stomp on the gas as hard as you can and see how far and accurately your truck can fling TV parts. Maybe you can flip some TV bits clear across the street and onto the neighbor's lawn. We call this maneuver the "news flash" and it will definitely reduce your stress.

Stress-relieving strategy #3

Find a massage table. Now, lay on your stomach with your elbows underneath you, all the while allowing your feet to rest completely relaxed. As the masseuse is giving you a soothing foot rub, gaze down the barrel of your loaded12-gauge shotgun, until you have your computer clearly in your sights. Then, gently squeeze the trigger. As the smoke clears and as small objects finish falling from the sky, if you're quiet enough, you should be able to hear birds chirping. You'll see leaves swaying in the breeze, or rain falling through the large hole in your former computer and believe me, you will feel the stress symbolically blast through your computer and dissipate into the ether. You will now reach a stage of perfect peace, contentment, and relaxation knowing that your computer is finally having it's turn experiencing what we now call a "MEGA BITE." You will have experienced "mega bite therapy" and will feel much, much better.

Worry #21
What if I turn myself into the IRS and have to act as my own attorney?

 # Exercise Relieving Stresses

It has been proven that exercise can relieve stress[1]. If this is true, then according to the commutative law of humanity[2], the opposite is also true. Stress must relieve exercise. This is an important revelation for people who are sick and tired of working harder than a three-legged sled-dog while going nowhere on a stationary bicycle or who every day feel guilty if they don't spend an hour dodging SUVs in their spandex

---

[1]Actually, we are putting this footnote here because, technically speaking, we're not sure this has been proven. We think we heard this somewhere though, and from somebody who seemed to know what they were talking about. To provide journalistic accuracy we should probably also point out that, statistically speaking, it has also been proven that weasels could have engineered the pyramids.

[2]Or is it the Pythagorean theorem? We certainly don't know.

and helmet, or who, because of their race, religion, or alien planet of origin, conscientiously refuse to exercise on moral grounds – because they would rather watch TV. These people should be happy to know that one of the main benefits of stress is relief from exercise.

Following this logic out to it's conclusion, if you are one who is stressed to the point that your brain feels like a guppy in a tank of barracudas, then, you are also one who should strive for a high degree of stress in order to relieve yourself of the need to exercise. The following are 10 obvious examples of ways to greatly increase your stress so as to significantly reduce your level of exercise:

1. Make a career change to air traffic controller or junior high shop teacher.

2. Turn yourself in to the I.R.S. and act as your own attorney.

3. Use stage makeup to paint bruises and cuts on your small children before you send them to school each day.

4. Make a regular habit of watching the evening news.

5. Borrow all the money you can from organized crime friends on the street and spend it all on state lottery tickets.

6. Join a terrorist organization and brag to everyone you see how you're sticking it to the U.S. Government.

7. Build your house just below a dam or on a steep incline prone to mudslides.

8. Spend a considerable amount of time driving on the streets around your local high school.

9. Sink your entire life savings into Alpaca futures or into Al Gore's latest presidential campaign.

10. Own and operate a small business.

Worry #5911
How many calories am I burning
while I stand here?

 Questions
from Worried
Drivers

One major cause of stress is driving on roads infested with idiots. Since I am the best driver I personally know, to me, the problem is obvious. There are too darned many idiots out there. Fortunately for the rest of you frustrated motorists, you have me and my amazing driving expertise to solve your problem. I believe that it might be possible to rehabilitate some of these idiots if we could just get them some additional instruction.

If you think about it, most of us got our drivers training at a time in our lives when we were generally distracted and so most of it was never absorbed into our brains. When you're a teenager, aside from generally never paying attention, there were way too many fun things to do. Seriously, if you're a drivers Ed teacher, how do you compete with planning to toss a dead skunk into the middle of your rival high school's prom, or with daydreams of some hot babe or guy, or with music by bands with names like Rancid Mucous? So, for those of you rotten drivers out there, we are here to answer your questions.

Questions from Rotten Drivers

Question:
Biff Birdwell from Weasel Falls, Colorado writes, "I often use a technique I was taught as a young driver known as the "rolling stop." I have been wondering, is this technique currently being taught in drivers Ed courses, and how do most law enforcement officials feel about it?"

Answer:
For those readers who might not be aware, the rolling stop is a technique designed by armchair traffic engineers to speed up traffic. It has also been proven to conserve precious resources like tire rubber and non-renewable transmissions. The rolling stop is best used at STOP signs when you know they are only joking.

By the way, it sounds like you hadn't heard, but Drivers' Ed the way you know it is no longer taught in high schools. The schools figure now days, young people get enough training on skateboards and by playing video games.

Question:

Speaking of only joking, Martha from Washington writes, "My husband insists that the 55 mile per hour speed limit sign is a big joke. Judging by the way most people drive, I have to agree with him. If that's the case, what is the real speed limit?

Answer:

Never drive faster than your guardian angel can fly is a trite, over-used cliche' that is actually pretty accurate. Certainly, driving 55 can be extraordinarily dangerous. What a tragedy if you're out loafing along at 55 M.P.H. and some other innocent driver were to be killed by a stray bullet shot at you by some other frustrated driver.

Question:

Will Knapp from Euphoria Falls, Canada writes, "At times when I find myself creeping along behind a real wienerhead. How close can I get to the guy in front of me? Would nudging him along with my bumper be the most civic minded way to help move him along?"

Answer:

Yes

Question:

Sue Cabesa from Crusted Butte, Wyoming asks, "For times when another driver is being a real jerk, but you aren't sure whether or not he is dangerous, do you know of a hand sign I can make which will show my contempt for the other driver, yet not risk being offensive or allow his lawyer to plea-bargain his sentence down to manslaughter?"

Answer:

Dear Sue, being a woman, you can get away with nearly any hand sign if you just put a big happy smile on your face. In fact, at times, even more effective than hand signs are large posters, which you can hang out the window. The advantage of posters is that you can have a whole bunch made up in advance. Then, you can choose just the right one that will make it very clear to the other driver precisely why he or she is a jerk. An alternative to hand signs or posters which will show your contempt toward all other divers generally is to skip driving altogether and ride public transportation... and display a rubber chicken.

Things a flag person should be worried about

1. What if the next driver doesn't stop?

2. What if the next driver is asleep?

3. What if the next driver is blind?

4. What if the next driver just died of a heart attack and fell across his steering wheel with all his weight on the gas pedal?

5. What if I grabbed a salami this morning instead of a stop sign? What if this thing I'm holding IS a salami?

6. What if the next driver wants to joust with me?

7. What if one of these drivers is delusional and thinks this sign is a gun?

8. How many calories am I burning while I stand here?

9. What other job does this qualify me to do?

Some things a pilot car driver should be worried about:

1. What if nobody follows me?

2. What if I get lost?

3. What if these drivers are menopausal?

4. What if these drivers are delusional and think this sign is an alien?

5. What if immigration thinks I'm trying to run away?

6. Will I get fired if I drive off a cliff and 100 cars follow me?

7. What if another driver wants to race?

8. What if my employer finds out that these other drivers are capable of finding their way through the construction without me?

Things a paranoid schizophrenic driver will worry about:

1. Which one of these cars am I driving?

2. What was that noise?

3. What if my airbag goes off when I run into me?

4. What was that noise?

5. Why am I driving be hind me in that car with the red and blue flashing lights and the rubber truck escort?

6. What was that noise?

7. What if these yellow stripes have feelings?

8. What was that noise?

10 Lying can cause Worry and Stress

Life just isn't fair. For example, regardless of how much you would like to, and in spite of how right-on-the-money accurate it is, you can't call a filthy, disgusting, depraved, unprincipled, lawyer a crook or a liar in public. You could get sued for defamation of a character. So you must lie. You are left to describe him using a milk toast, politically correct term like "ethically challenged or "honesty disadvantaged," and you must call him "Esq." all the while worrying that you will still get sued.

When your sister in law has been slaving over a hot stove all day to make her special sweet-and-sour liver casserole, you can't grab your throat, flop on the floor, gag, choke, and accuse her of trying to poison you. To keep from being ostracized by your in-laws, you must lie. You mumble, "It's terrific!" as your bulging eyes search the room for a plant to receive some biodegradable material. And then you must worry that you will start liking this stuff.

It's just not fair that when a cop pulls you over for speeding you can't just blurt out the truth. You can't say "Yes, I was speeding, and as soon as you're out of sight I'll be cruising along again at the speed limit plus 20, only next time I'll be looking farther ahead toward the horizon... and he can't be honest with you either, because if he was, he would admit that "this silly speed limit is not about our safety. We don't give a hoot about your safety. Everybody knows these artificially low speed limits are all about revenue, and I haven't met my quota yet, otherwise I would be relaxing at the donut shop waiting for a call on a domestic disturbance or actually driving with traffic." No, we can't say those things; we have to lie, which causes stress.

Conjuring up lies is so stressful. Even your friends hate doing it. I'm trying to be as diplomatic as I can when I say this, but you're not the only one who lies like a rug. Your friends and acquaintances are regularly lying to you too. Luckily, you've got me to help straighten things out. We're going to start right now.

The truth about your life

You may not be the best driver on the road. It's true. In fact, more than likely, you are a rotten driver. Your driving is not a marvel and example to others. To all the other drivers on the road, you are a jerk. The drivers who DON'T flip you off should. They lie because they're afraid that if they did flip you off you would ram them and their car is quite a bit more expensive than yours.

You are not all that funny. You are pretty much the only one who thinks so. Most everybody else thinks your witticisms are about as sharp as a clam's teeth, and about as bright as a flashlight with 10-year-old batteries.

She is not "OK." That is a big lie. In fact, as you will eventually figure out, she's as mad as heck at you because you did not properly interpret her silence, body language, dilating pupils, and pheromone reduction so that you would know that when she said "yes" what she really meant was "no." Any phool could figure that out.

Everybody hates your dog. All those people who smile and say "It's OK" when he sniffs their crotches, digs up their flowers, and jumps up leaving tracks on their pants, they're all lying. The only one who thinks it's cute is you, and the pictures you took make you look like an idiot.

Your cat is not cute either. It's obnoxious. So is the souvenir fur that you send home clinging to everyone's clothes.

No one is impressed with how smart you are. They only one who thinks you're brilliant is you. Everyone else thinks you're annoying, especially the smiling, glassy-eyed students in your college classes. If they told you what they really thought, you would flunk them, which is why they will call me a liar.

See. We lie. Doesn't knowing that relieve your stress?

Some things a pecan pie should be worried about:

1. What is that lady doing with that knife?

2. What kind of future life will I have?

3. Am I something which, when cut into pieces, each piece will generate a new creature?

4. I'm not?

5. What must people think about something filled with nuts?

6. What does a pastry do for fun?

7. Will me "in the face" be funny?

8. What if I ever need to DO something; how does that work?

9. If someone drops me, will I land upside down?

 11   The Truth About Life, Worry, and Stress

Note: Knowing the truth about life can either cause more stress and worry, as in the case of knowing that the blizzard of the century will be burying the mountains during your drive to Aunt Mildred's funeral, or it can actually reduce stress, as in the case of knowing that the majority of voters are more than 14 years old, don't smoke dope, and can readily see that Cheryl Crowe and Jane Fonda are imbeciles.

Since way out here on our end, we can't usually tell which bit of information will relieve your stress and which ones will cause you to worry, we are just going to act like typical journalists and try to get you to buy our book so we can make a whole lot of money. If this causes you to worry about the state of journalism, we hope at least you enjoy it.

Oh, yes, and go ahead and stress if you want to, but it won't do any good because here is the truth about life.

The truth about life

-Success comes to those who are too busy to enjoy it.

-Elvis is dead. So is Santa Clause.

-You will never be as popular as beer or sleep.

-Even if they ask you in a cheery voice, nobody really cares, "how you're doing."

-The good things that come to those who wait are pretty much what's left over from those who got there earlier.

-"Let's get together sometime" really means: "This conversation will be all the contact I need with you for at least another 10 years."

-You are pretty much the only person who actually takes you seriously-unless you have something people want.

-YOU will never win the lottery.

-If, against all reasonable odds, you did happen to win the lottery, and after you finished piddling away all that money, you know perfectly well that you will wind up in worse shape than you were before. You will be miserable and, to add to your troubles, everyone will hate you.

-The financial infrastructure of the entire world is little more than an enormous display of smoke and mirrors teetering on top of a house of cards.

-Because people like you really know how to have fun, you will never have the money to do it.

-If you really do, "have a nice day," there are scads of people who will immediately become envious and go to work to ruin it for you.

-The way to live longer is to give up all the things that make you want to live longer.

-More money will make public schools better just like more gas will make your clunker car faster and more reliable.

-Beautiful people can wear nearly anything and look great. You, on the other hand, should probably work towards looking "normal."

-You can't successfully blame the smell on somebody else if there are only two of you in the elevator.

-Fair is where you take your pigs.

-Except for war, football or video games, if you want something done right, ask a woman.

-Sadly, deep down inside you know that the only way to really look better and be healthier is to exercise regularly and change your diet.

-Success generally only comes to those people who are really into things you hate doing.

-Your dog doesn't love you. He acts that way purely on instinct because it gets him what he wants. He could just as easily have been conditioned to eat you.

-Your cat takes you for granted and, when all is said and done is every bit as loyal to you as a typical pro athlete is to his team.

-When you boil it all down, happiness or unhappiness is 100% your choice.

-The only way for us to have a better world is for each of us, individually, to be a better person.

Legitimate things for a humor writer to be worried about:

1. Will I be ridiculed in the academic community for regularly ending sentences with prepositions?

2. What if the stuffy, self-important literature critics start writing good stuff about my books?

3. What if cat owners, political activists, leaders of womens' organizations, self-appointed minority leaders and bureaucrats suddenly develop a sense of humor?

4. If my blood pressure makes the Guiness book of world records, would that be a good thing or a bad thing?

5. What if nobody but me thinks this stuff I'm writing is funny?

Something Unrelated

There are some of my readers who would say that this chapter has nothing whatsoever to do with the idea of worrying. These are obviously people who never had to come up with enough entertaining material to fill a complete book. So I would say to them, "lighten up; don't stress." In our quest for absolute journalistic accuracy we add this disclaimer: **This chapter has very little to do with worrying. So what.**

Corporate Slogans

The two or three of you out there who follow my books and who have enough eyesight left to read the fine print on the back covers know what an awful time we've had over the years coming up with a trendy corporate slogan. There are many reasons for this. Besides a general inability to make decisions which is most apparent on really important stuff like whether or not to fight my speeding ticket or how soon to start taking my cholesterol medication after my kidney stones, there's also the fact that I'm not a corporation, just a guy. Of course, we also struggle with my wife, Robyn's integrity. She insists that we can't mislead the public. I don't know how she thinks we are ever going to sell any books.

The bottom line: After 10 years, it's time we had a permanent slogan the public can get sick of hearing so they can associate our company with redundancy, tedium, and being annoyed. So, we decided to let you, our readers decide. You can register your vote by logging onto our web site. Your vote will be counted as soon as you have placed a minimum order of 1000 books. Each option is clearly numbered to help our slower readers or those who can't read at all. Some of you will easily be able to spot the slogans I came up with. Don't let that influence your decision.

A gaggle of possible Apricot Press slogans

-Apricot Press, our books will make you better looking.

-Apricot Press, better than a losing lottery ticket.

-Apricot Press, probably the only company that wouldn't let fame and fortune go to it's head.

-Apricot Press, Selling books because doing surgery would get us into trouble.

-Apricot Press, Glad to see you if we don't owe you money.

-Apricot Press, If we didn't have to come to work, we would probably just get ourselves into trouble.

-Apricot Press, That's not how we remember it

-Apricot Press, you'll be glad you trusted your brain to us.

-Apricot Press, None of our money goes to support terrorists.

-Buy our books. We'll be glad you did.

-Apricot Press, Selling books because we're not licensed to practice law.

-Apricot Press, Selling books because we don't understand computers.

-Apricot Press, Selling books because we couldn't get into medical school.

-Apricot Press, This isn't as easy as it looks.

-Apricot Press, We probably haven't done half the stuff we've been accused of.

-Apricot Press, We still have too few assets to be sued.

-Apricot Press, Just saying no to drugs and scary movies.

-Apricot Press, Hoping to someday afford a new car.

-Apricot Press, Now don't get all huffy.

-Apricot Press, , Striving to dominate the literary world one joke at a time.

-Apricot Press, We're funny so you don't have to be.

-Apricot Press, Eventually paying most of our bills.

-Apricot Press, Let's see you do any better.

-We didn't see anything.

-Apricot Press, Adjusting our britches to better serve you.

-Apricot Press, Hoping to eventually make a profit.

-Apricot Press, So far unable to come up with any better ideas.

-Apricot Press, Wishing everyone liked us.

-Apricot Press, You've seen worse.

-Apricot Press, Even if you don't like our books, you can still buy them.

-Down with the media – except us.

-Apricot Press, Wishing we could afford to dress better.

-Apricot Press, Where books get shipped and laundry gets done all at the same time.

-Apricot Press, When we get tired of watching the clock, we take a nap.

-Apricot Press, Hoping we put the decimal in the right place.

-Apricot Press, Where you don't need facts to have an opinion.

-Apricot Press, Trying to appear incompetent in order to lull the competition to sleep.

Worry #9572
How does such a big egg get out?

 # The History of Worrying as We Know It

Not all that long ago, at least in astrophysicist years, we were pastoral people. There were no cars, cell-phones, deodorant, toilets, toilet paper, mouthwash, septic systems, personal hygiene products, or room fresheners. Life was simple – smelly, but simple. If a person wanted to talk to an old friend who lived far away... forget it. It was impossible. If somebody's kidneys were failing. They died because medicine hadn't been invented yet. If the weather had been rotten and the wild gooseberries were frozen, yet, somebody still wanted to eat. They ate rocks or tree bark. If a guy had never heard that smoking could be harmful to his health or was forced by cigarette advertisers kicking and screaming against his will to smoke 5 packs of cigarettes a day, so that he died from lung cancer, his problem was simple. His surviving relatives just had to go pick up a rock and smash the cigarette manufacturers over the head because political activist judges and corrupt lawyers hadn't been invented yet. "What does this have to do with worrying?" You ask. Frankly, we're not sure, but we hope that before we finish we can tie it all together.

Fast-forward to Egypt and the year 2000 B.C. Mrs. and Mr. Pharaoh are skateboarding down the pyramids and they fall off and break their royal necks because the skateboard manufacturer failed to place a label prominently on the skateboard warning that skating down the pyramids could be harmful to Pharaoh's and Pharaohettes. What can they do? Nothing. They are dead. Besides that, worrying techniques, just like civilization, were still in a primitive state. You see, life in those days was simple. Unlike today, boredom was pretty much the people's biggest problem. In fact, most scientists agree that The Sphinx was just a giant ceramic doodle and The Pyramids a big pile of rocks a bunch of construction guys stacked up when they were bored, so there was still not much stress, not even on the horizon mostly because the horizon was filled up with pyramids.

Forward again to AD 100. The Romans are feeding the Christians to the lions, fighting the barbarians for the love of it, and building huge water slides, which some nimrod modern archeologists have misidentified as aqueducts. Leprosy was rampant, plagues and

Cleopatra were ravishing, but epic stress and worry were still far in the future.

So you see, through all of known human history, clear up until 1776, people just didn't have much to worry about. Oh, sure, the British were occupying Boston, the Hessians were Hessioning around, patriots were fleeing through swamps or hanging out in Pennsylvania with rags on their feet, but nobody was getting all stressed about it. And this is pretty much the way things were clear up until modern times when the foul winds of change were beginning to break.

Breaking foul winds of change

Somehow, in the last few years, all of this changed. While the news reporters were all out looking for a new scandal, just as general what's-his-name was sweeping out the last military base getting ready to turn off the lights, just as the economy was headed into the tank, just as the last remaining foreign national was getting settled into his home in Tucson, the worm turned. Although VCRs, TV's, and Cell Phones, had all previously been invented, nobody cared! I know I didn't'. We were just having a big party. Even when Al Gore invented the Internet no one cared, only a hand full of really dweeby pencil-necks ever used it. However, deep in the shadows, out of the gaze of the partying public, with only a few whiny special interest lawyers watching, ominous waves were symbolically rolling toward the shore. Vital manufacturing technology was sold to the

Chinese in exchange for illegal campaign contributions. Within only days, Asian sweatshops began to produce Big Macs, computers, VCRs, DVDs, BVDs, and nuclear missiles so inexpensively that even starving public school teachers could buy them. Asian manufacturers were turning out palm pilots, SUVs, cell phones, singing wall trout, digital cameras, car bombs, and intercontinental ballistic missiles for as little as $5.00 with the mail in rebate! As you can imagine, life began to change rapidly. Before we knew it, innocent people were getting beeped by sales people in the middle of important phone calls, Spam was literally leaping out of our computer screens and into our cereal bowls, people in large numbers were watching the TV on their dashboard instead paying attention to the traffic lights so that when the light had cycled through 4 straight times, they thought the horns honking were on the Jackie Chan movie they were watching.

Life finally got so crazy that print cartridge refills made up nearly 70% of the gross national product. Profits from Beanie Babies were funding terrorism, and the national debt was nearly as large as some basketball players' jewelry budget. The politicians were dumfounded, which in and of itself is no big deal, but the rest of this stuff was clearly a recipe for disaster, the end to simplicity and mellowness as we know it and the beginning of the age of worry.

And now, for the first time in human history, people in large numbers are beginning to get serious about worrying. They worry about the future of their 401-K, they worry about health care for their pet, they worry that while nobody was paying attention, Hillary Clinton got elected to the Senate. The volume of worry in America began to spiral upward like a finger in a 3-year-old's nasal passage.

The state of stress and worry today

So, I don't have to tell you that in the world in which we live, stress and worry have become a part of life. We revel in it. We party in it. We work in it, we use it as a great excuse for doing stupid things, and we croak because of it. So now, the only thing left for us to do is to explain what to do about it, and ultimately, to make jokes about it, which we definitely plan to do in the remaining chapter.

Worry #873
Will the Cubs win the World Series this year?

14 The future of worry and stress

No one can say for certain what the future will bring; however, one thing is absolutely certain: people of the future will get all excited and pay big bucks to people who will go out on a limb and predict the future. Witness the goofy things people do because of a bogus horoscope. Check the circulation of tabloid newspapers! Observe what a celebrity Nostradamus has become and he's been dead for hundreds of years! So, despite the fact that my predictions are about as valid as an Elvis drivers license, I'm going to make them. Here is my shot at immortality.

First, it's a pretty safe bet that in the future people will find something to stress and worry about. If for no other reason than that it makes absolutely no sense whatsoever to worry and we have a world full of neurotic people who pretty much decide what they're going to do based upon that fact that it makes no sense. Therefore, we are pretty much guaranteed that there will be adequate worrying going on.

My next prediction is that the Cubs will not win the World Series this season—or next season—or the one after that. This needs no explanation.

For my third prediction, I am predicting that the world will not end any time soon. If I'm wrong, I'm sure I will I hear it from some of you sore heads on this one.

And, finally, I prophesy that this book will improve the QUALITY of worrying worldwide, in case you weren't worried about the future, here's some great stuff to get you moving in that direction. Some of you will want to start right now.

Another clot of future things to worry about

Since I am now an expert on predicting the future, when I win the lottery, will the people who I thought were my friends hate me out of jealousy?

When we finally make contact with alien beings, will they know of something worthwhile to watch on TV?

When sports figures and celebrities finally have ALL of the money, will THEY pay for the summer time road construction, and how will we buy tickets?

After I'm gone, will anybody out there be left who is competent to properly poke fun at cats?

When all the research is finally in on health and nutrition, what if there really is nothing safe to eat?

When the fringe kooks complete their takeover of the world and vegetarianism becomes the law, will cows, pigs, and chickens become endangered?

Help me on this one. I can't think of any more.

'The Truth About Life' Humor Books